Enter here!

This year you will be entering the amazing worlds of FLUENCY and LEGIBILITY.

You will develop speed and rhythm.

You will develop confidence and pride in your handwriting ability.

JOB APPLICATION: HANDWRITING EXPLORER

Name: ______________________________

Date of birth: ______________________________

Previous handwriting experience: ______________________________

____

____

AF584723

Why I would make a good handwriting explorer: ______________________________

____

____

Trace then write.

A wise old owl sat in an oak.

The more he heard the less he spoke.

The less he spoke the more he heard.

Why aren't we all like that wise old bird?

Trace then write the capital letters.

A B C D E F G H I J K L M

N O P Q R S T U V W X Y Z

Handwriting: lower-case and upper-case (capital) printing. **Grammar:** statement; question; sentences. **Punctuation:** upper-case (capital) letters to start sentences; full stops; question mark. **Spelling and vocabulary:** rhyme (heard/bird, oak/spoke). **Literary elements**: Mother Goose rhyme.

Trace then write.

Little Robin Redbreast

sat upon a rail;

Niddle noddle went its head.

Wiggle waggle went its tail.

Make sure letters with tails (descenders) and tall letters (ascenders) slope evenly, too.

Trace then write the punctuation marks.

“ ” , ; : ? ! _ “ ” , ; : ? ! _

Trace then write.

“Oooh! Oooh!” exclaimed the owl.

“What did you say?” asked the robin.

Trace then write.

1 2 3 4 5 6 7 8 9 10 1 2 3 4 5 6 7 8 9 10

Self assessment

My ascenders and descenders slope evenly:

sometimes ☐ often ☐ always ☐.

Handwriting: lower-case and upper-case (capital) printing; introducing terminology (descenders and ascenders); punctuation; numerals. **Grammar:** statement; exclamation; question; saying verbs (exclaimed, asked). **Punctuation:** sentence punctuation; quotation marks; exclamation marks; question marks. **Spelling and vocabulary:** rhyme (rail/tail). **Literary elements**: onomatopoeia; Mother Goose rhyme.

Choose an adjective and a noun for each label. Remember to print.

Adjective	awesome, fearsome, loathsome, cumbersome, troublesome, handsome, gruesome
Noun	teeth, jaws, scales, legs, tail, claws, eyes

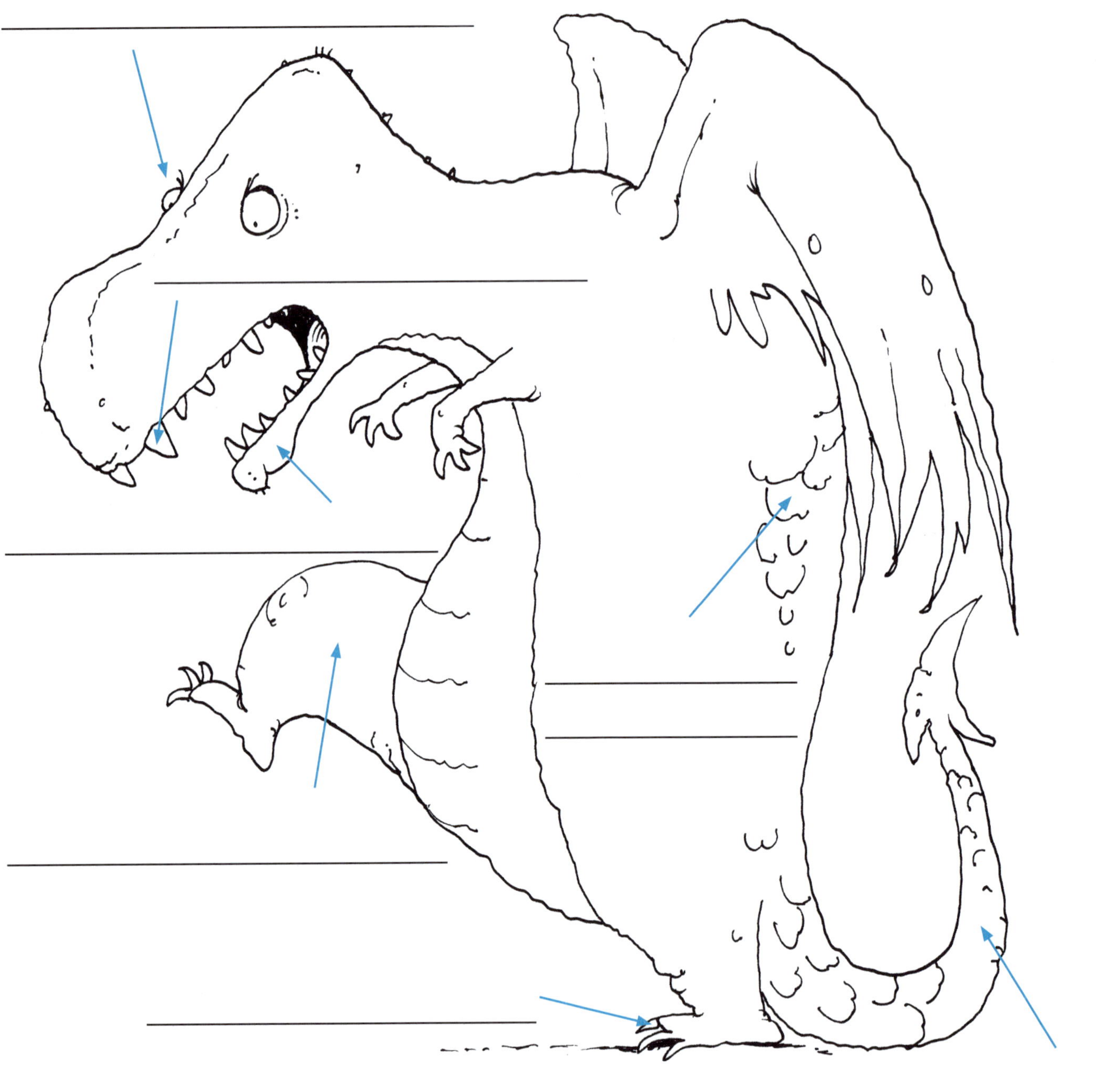

Label any extra parts you like. Give the creature a name.

Handwriting: using printing to label diagrams. **Spelling and vocabulary:** suffix -some. **Literary elements**: mythical creatures (dragons, beasts).

Use a diagonal join . . .	
from any of these letters a c d e h i k l m n t u x	to any of these rounded entries. m n r x z

a	→	a	→	an
Make an exit . . .		then keep going up . . .		until you get to the rounded entry.

Trace then write.

am en im in an em un um

knee knock know knight knew

ax ux ix ex az ez iz uz ar ir

mix exciting excellent exhilarating

exhaust pixie solemn artist thirst

dream cream stream team lean

You're barking up

the wrong tree.

Handwriting: diagonal joins to rounded entries. **Spelling and vocabulary**: digraph 'ea' (stream, cream); silent k (knee, knock); silent n (solemn).

Review: Diagonal joins to pointed entries

from any of these letters	to any of these pointed entries.
a c d e h i k l m n t u x	i j p u v w y

Trace then write. Remember to make smooth diagonal joins.

ai ai aj aj ay au av aw ai ai

ap ci ci cu cu du di ei ap ci

ep ep eu eu ew ev hi hu ep ep

hu hy ip ij ep ki ku ky hu hy

ky mi mp mu my ni nu ny ky

ny ti tu ty xi xp xu xy ny ti

Every cloud has a silver lining.

Circle your smoothest join.
Underline a join that needs more practice.

Handwriting: diagonal joins to pointed entries. **Spelling**: common letter pairs. **Literary elements**: idiom.

Use a diagonal join . . .	
from any of these letters a c d e h i k l m n t u x	to any of these tall letters. b h k l t

a → a/ → al

Make an exit . . . then keep going up all the way . . . then retrace to make the next letter.

To join from an exit to a tall letter, keep going up and then retrace.

Trace then write. Be careful when you retrace the join.

ab ah al ak at cl ch ck

ct dt dl dh el et eb ht

hl ik il it ib kl kh ll lk kl

lt mb ml nb nh nt nk nl nb

th tt tl uk ub ut ul at it th

get into hot water

pick of the litter

Pick me!

Self assessment

My retracing to make joins is:

improving ☐ good ☐ fantastic ☐.

Handwriting: diagonal joins to ascenders. **Spelling**: common letter pairs. **Literary elements**: idiom.

Review: Diagonal joins to o and e

Use a diagonal join . . .	
to o or e	from any of these letters. a c d e h i k l m n t u x

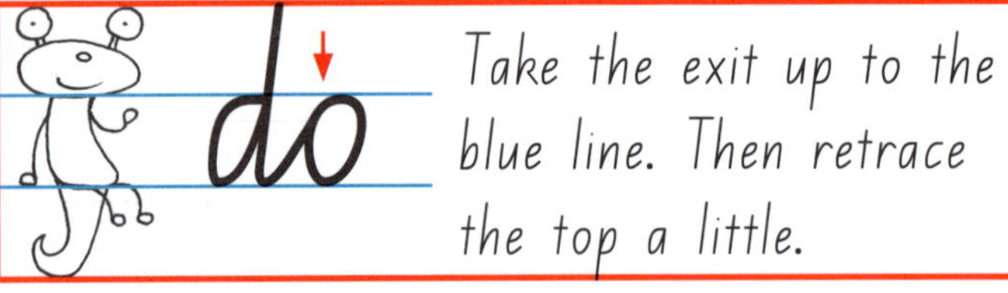

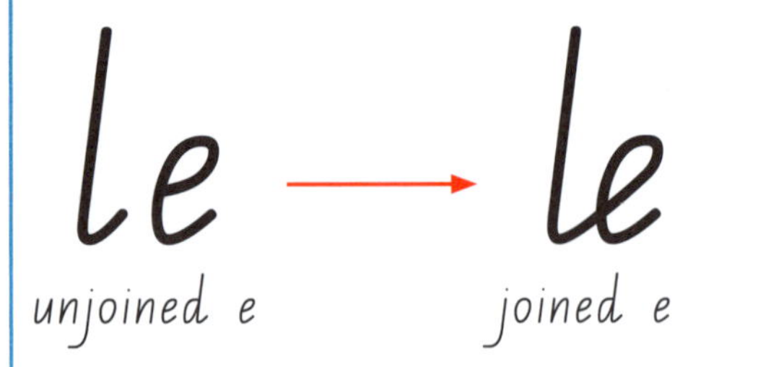

Trace then write.

co do ho lo mo no lo ko co do ho lo

ce de ee he ie ke le me ce de ee he ie

ne te ue xe ce de ee he ie ne te ue xe

co do ho lo mo no lo ko co do ho lo

belief believe believing believable unbelievable

It's a piece of cake.

He thinks he's the bee's knees.

Handwriting: diagonal joins to o and e. **Grammar:** sentences; apostrophe for possession (bee's). **Spelling and vocabulary**: word families (belief, believe); apostrophe for contraction (it's, he's). **Literary elements**: idiom.

Write the downstroke. Lift your pencil and start the crossbar low enough to angle up to the next letter.

Trace then write.

fa fa fa

fi fi fi

fo fo fo

fu fu fu

fr fr fr

fy fy fy

fl fl fl

piffle sniffle wiffle waffle

fly flip flop flash flow

freeze fry fiddle flew float follow factual

funny friendly fresh frozen frosty frightened

Handwriting: joins from f; joining to a and to o; joining along the crossbar. **Grammar**: verbs, adjectives. **Literary elements**: onomatopoeia.

Review: Joins to and from f

a → af → afe

Write the letter and go up.

Then make a small loop to go down.

Lift your pencil and use the crossbar to join to the next letter.

Using a loop to join to f means you don't have to retrace.

Double f has two loops!

off

Use the crossbar to loop to the second f.

Trace then write.

uf uf

ef ef

af af

of of

lf lf

if if

df df

rf rf

Trace then write. Remember to join the second f from the first crossbar.

off off

Trace then write.

loafing swift dreadful unsafe awful boxfish

wolf oaf elf waif chief shelf

sniff huff puff bluff surf drift

The awful wolf huffed and puffed.

Self assessment

I remembered to slope the crossbar on f to suit the letter that follows: sometimes ☐ often ☐ always ☐.

Handwriting: joins to f. **Grammar**: adjectives; nouns; verbs; noun group (The awful wolf); past tense. **Spelling and vocabulary**: common letter pairs; rhyme (huff/puff/bluff, swift/drift). **Literary elements**: reference to folk tale (the Three Pigs).

Trace then write.

Four friends ate fresh fried fly fritters.

Fearless Flo flew to France on Friday.

The furry fly flitted through fifty flowers.

Five frantic frogs fled from fifty fierce fishes.

A fly and a flea flew into a flue, said
the fly to the flea, "What shall we do?"
"Let us fly," said the flea.
Said the fly, "Shall we flee?"
So they flew through a flaw in the flue.

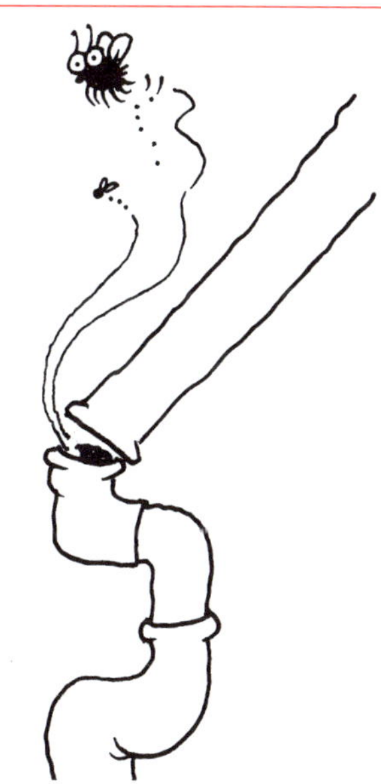

Write the tongue twister.

Handwriting: joins to and from f. **Grammar:** sentences; questions; proper nouns (France, Friday, Flo); prepositional phases (into the flue, through a flaw); doing verbs. **Punctuation:** quotation marks; commas; question marks. **Literary elements:** alliteration; tongue twisters.

Review: Dropping on letters

a	→ a	→ ac
Make an exit . . .	then keep going up . . .	pencil lift — lift your pencil and drop on the letter.

Use exits from any of these letters	to drop on any of these letters.
a c d e h i k l m n t u x	a c d g q

Trace the letter pairs. Remember to draw a longer exit.

ma ma na na uc ic ud id ca da ma ma na na uc

uq iq ug ig ng nd nc nd ug iq uq iq ug ig ng nd

la la ta ha ha ka ka ld ad ac la la ta ha ha ka ld

Trace then write.

The ugly duckling turned into a swan.

Only a true Princess can feel a pea beneath

20 mattresses and 20 featherbeds.

Handwriting: dropping on letters. **Punctuation:** sentence punctuation. **Spelling and vocabulary**: plurals adding -s or –es; animal young (ducklings, cygnet). **Literary elements:** references to fairy tales ('The Ugly Duckling', 'The Princess and the Pea' by Hans Christian Andersen).

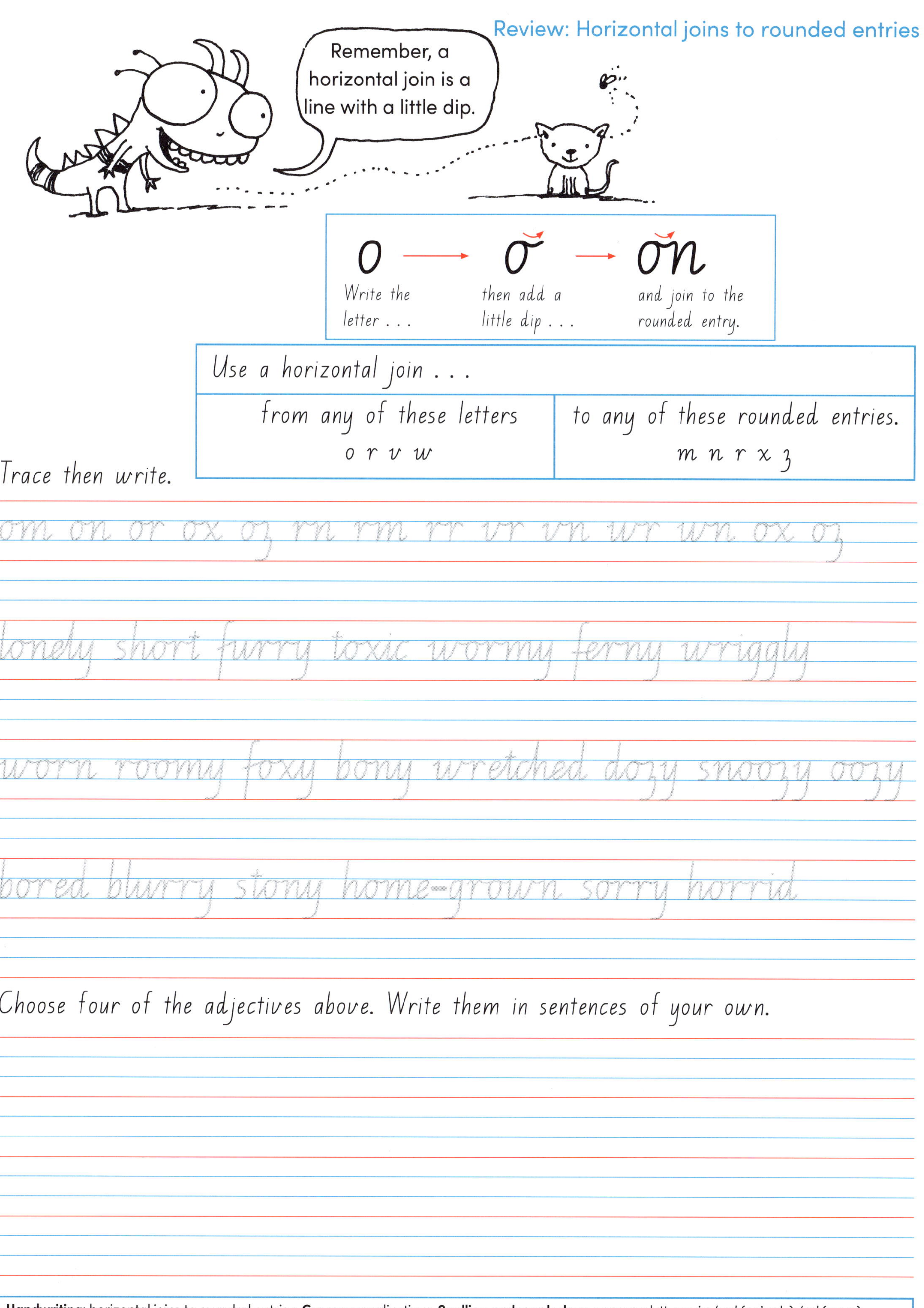

o → o → on

Write the letter . . . then add a little dip . . . and join to the rounded entry.

Use a horizontal join . . .	
from any of these letters o r v w	to any of these rounded entries. m n r x z

Trace then write.

om on or ox oz rn rm rr vr vn wr wn ox oz

lonely short furry toxic wormy ferny wriggly

worn roomy foxy bony wretched dozy snoozy oozy

bored blurry stony home-grown sorry horrid

Choose four of the adjectives above. Write them in sentences of your own.

Handwriting: horizontal joins to rounded entries. **Grammar**: adjectives. **Spelling and vocabulary**: common letter pairs 'wr' (wriggly), 'or' (worn).

Review: Horizontal joins to pointed entries

Use a horizontal join . . .	
from any of these letters o r v w	to any of these pointed entries. i j p u v w y

Trace then write.

oy oy op op oj ow ow op ry ry ru ru ri ri rp rw

vy vu vi vi vu vu vy vu oi ov op ow oy ou oi

ri rp rv ry oi op wi wy wi wi wu wy wy

wy wavy vulture vine showy harp larva

Trace then write.

burps like a yowie

wriggles like a widget

Self assessment Circle your five best diagonal joins.

Handwriting: horizontal joins to pointed entries. **Spelling and vocabulary:** digraph 'ur' (burp). The word *yowie* is from the Yuwaalaraay language. **Literary elements**: similes.

Circle your five best horizontal joins.

Handwriting: horizontal joins to ascenders. **Grammar:** adjectives (spooky, weird, dark); adverb (very, horribly); compound sentence with coordinating conjunction (and); suffixes -ly, -ful, -ish, -less. **Spelling and vocabulary:** digraphs 'ow', 'oo', 'ir', 'ur', 'ar', 'ur'. **Literary elements**: alliteration (howled horribly); fantasy settings/scary genre; quote from *The Wonderful Wizard of Oz* by L Frank Baum (1900).

Review: Horizontal joins to anticlockwise letters

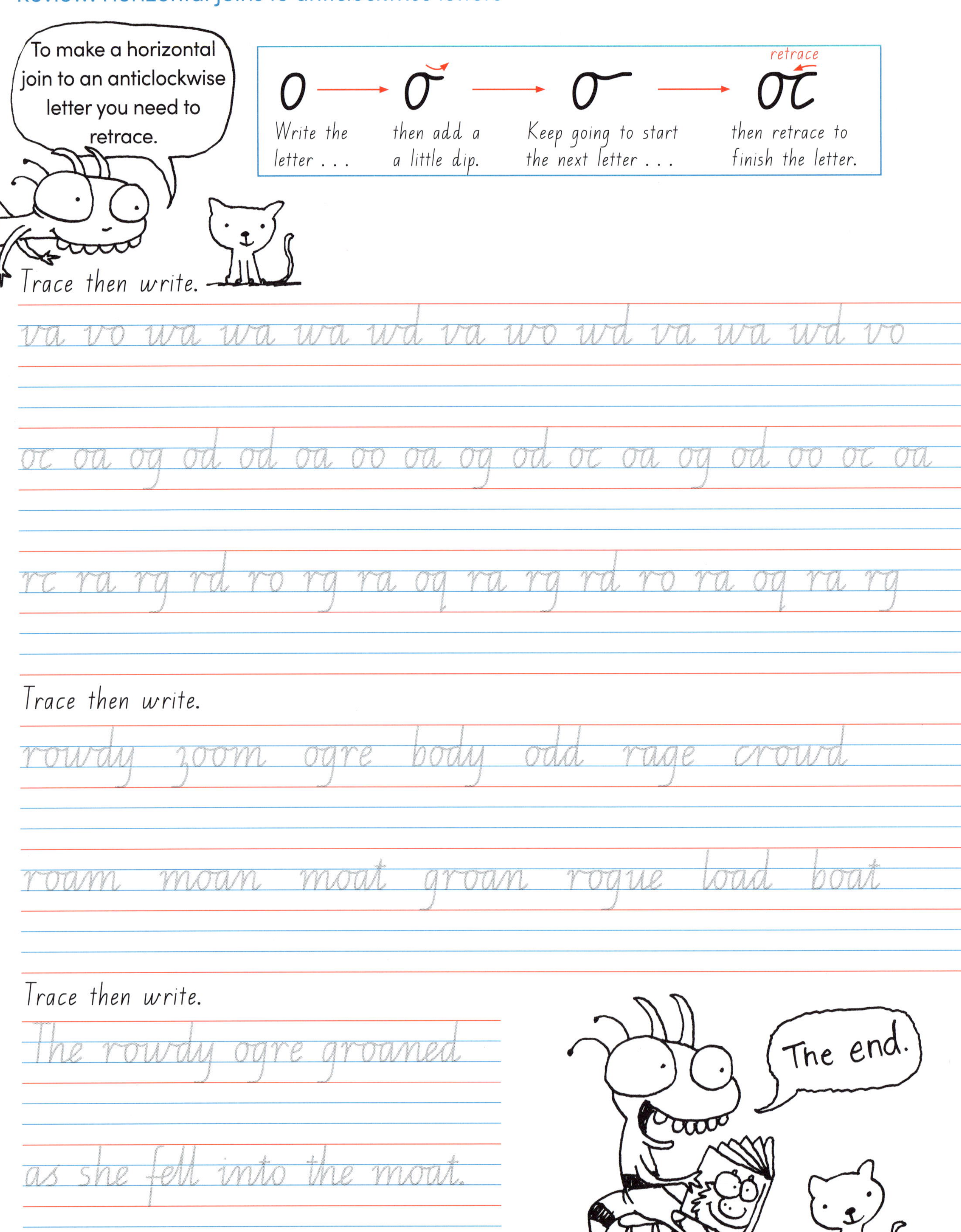

Handwriting: horizontal joins to anticlockwise letters a, c, d, g, o, q. **Grammar:** sentences. **Spelling and vocabulary:** digraphs 'ow' (rowdy, crowd), 'oa' (groan, moat, moan, toad, boat). **Literary elements**: fantasy character (ogre) and setting (moat); gender representation (she).

Handwriting: horizontal joins to s. **Punctuation:** sentence punctuation; quotation marks; proper noun (Sam). **Grammar:** adverbs ending in –ly; modal adverb (possibly). **Spelling and vocabulary**: suffix –ly (possibly, positively, loosely, mostly, crossly); rhyme (jaws, gnaws); silent g (gnaws).

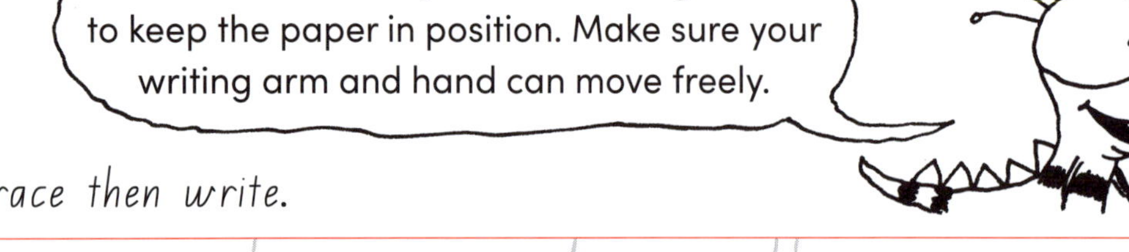

Trace then write.

pianos banjos solos cellos sopranos kilos

mangos avocados autos limos kangaroos

pose grows shows follows fellows

teachers cleaners managers smugglers

doctors plumbers gardeners authors

moss post whose nose utmost rose

course coarse thirst first juniors radars

Handwriting: horizontal joins to s. **Spelling and vocabulary**: mangos, mangoes, avocados and avocadoes are all correct; homophones (course/coarse); musical terms ending in o just add 's' (pianos); jobs often end in 'er', 'or' or 'ist' (cleaners, dentists). The word *kangaroo* is based on the word gangurru from the Guugu Yimithirr language.

Trace then write.

as as as as as as as as as as as peas

is is is is is is is is is is is is is fish

ns ns ns ns ns ns ns ns ns ns beans

ls ls ls ls ls ls ls ls ls ls ls ls ls trolls

ts ts ts ts ts ts ts ts ts ts ts ts ts hats

es es es es es es es es es es es es shoes

Trolls wearing hats and shoes ate

fish with peas and beans.

Self assessment

Tick any diagonal joins to s that are excellent.
Underline any joins that you could improve.

Handwriting: diagonal joins to s; modified s. **Grammar:** prepositional phrase (with peas and beans).

Review: Joins to s

Practise diagonal joins with these plurals. Trace then write.

snakes lizards walruses prizes

Trace then write.

fs fs fs fs fs fs fs fs fs fs fs fs fs fs fs fs

roofs cliffs reefs advisors

loaves thieves knives

hooves elves calves

Remember to pause if you need to and relax your hold on the pen or pencil.

Trace then write.

"The time has come," the Walrus said,

"To talk of many things:

Of shoes – and ships – and sealing-wax –

Of cabbages – and kings."

Handwriting: diagonal joins to s; modified s. **Punctuation:** sentence punctuation; quotation marks. **Spelling and vocabulary**: plurals adding –s, –es. **Literary elements:** quote from *Through the Looking Glass* by Lewis Carroll (1872).

Trace then write.

cc

dd

oo

ll

mm

nn

ee

rr

tt

ff

Practise joining these double letters. For oo you need to retrace a little. For cc and dd you need to drop on the second letter.

Remember that tt has a double crossbar.

Trace then write.

accepting adding stooping pulling humming

running sleeping stirring hitting puffing

Write some words of your own for the double letters that join together.

Underline any joins that you could improve.

Handwriting: double letters that join together. **Grammar:** verbs; tense; suffixes for tense -ing require a helper verb (is accepting, was adding). **Spelling and vocabulary**: double final consonant to add –ing (hit/hitting, run/running).

Review: Letters that join together

Trace then write these compound words.

overall wallpaper overrun waterproof treetop

strawberry rattlesnake toadstool seaweed

jellyfish sheepdog kneecap seagull foolproof

hummingbird toothbrush moonbeam goodnight

Trace then write the similes.

A cat's purr is beautiful,

like a strange lullaby.

Prrrrrr . . . Prrrrrr . . .

A cat's purr feels

like a car's motor running.

Handwriting: double letters that join together. **Grammar**: possessive apostrophes (cat's, car's). **Punctuation:** ellipsis (. . .). **Spelling and vocabulary:** compound words. **Literary elements:** similes; quote from *The Five Lives of our Cat Zook* by Joanne Rocklin (2012).

Trace then write.

yi ye yo ji ja ju ze zz

ba be bo bu bi br by pa pe pi

pn po pr pu py sa sc se si sa

sm sn so sp sq su sw sy so su sm sn

bl ph pl sh sk sl st bl pl sh bl ph pl

Letters that end in a clockwise direction (b, g, j, p, s, y and z) don't join to the next letter.

GLUE

Trace then write.

yolk yellow yell jam jumble zebra puzzle yacht

Trace then write the anagram pairs.

blame amble bear bare

please elapse pastel staple

Trace then write your own anagram.

bowl post seal

Handwriting: letters that end in a clockwise direction (b, g, j, p, s, y, z) don't join to the next letter. **Grammar:** homophones (bear, bare). **Spelling and vocabulary:** common letter pairs. **Literary elements:** anagrams.

Review: Letters that don't join

Remember, you can choose to join s to s, if the first s shape has changed.

oss iss

It's easier if you let double ss's be twins.

Trace then write the adjectives. Notice the letters that aren't joined.

missing bossy beautiful brilliant fussy glowing

gorgeous gassy green giggly gaudy jaunty

jealous juicy jagged jiggly mossy precious

pink pongy paltry pungent pretty putrid

petty happy stripy slimy sassy sensational

shaggy sloppy yellow yoghurty yummy yucky

Write some sentences using the adjectives above.

Handwriting: letters that end in a clockwise direction (b, g, j, p, s, y, z) don't join to the next letter. **Grammar:** adjectives; sentences. **Spelling and vocabulary**: rhyme (jiggly/giggly, saggy/shaggy); suffix –ful (beautiful, skilful).

oe re ve we

Trace then write.

oe re ve we re oe re ve we ve oe re ve we re oe re

oe re ve we we oe re ve we re oe re ve we we oe

arrive swerve delve love solve dissolve shove

believe deceive receive leave contrive heave

we're were weren't does doesn't have haven't

Trace then write.

"The werewolf doesn't exist,"

remarked the man.

Handwriting: letters that don't join to e (o, r, v, w). **Punctuation:** sentence punctuation; quotation marks. **Grammar:** verbs; saying verb (remarked). **Spelling and vocabulary**: apostrophes for contraction (we're, weren't, doesn't, haven't). **Literary elements**: reference to *The Bunyip of Berkeley's Creek* by Jenny Wagner and illustrated by Ron Brooks (1973).

Remember! z finishes in a clockwise direction, so it doesn't join to the next letter.

Trace then write.

ze zi zl zu zy zz zz ze zy zo za ze zy

sneeze wheeze freeze breeze squeeze tweezers

Look! q doesn't join to u.

Write your own words that use z.

Trace then write.

qu qu qu qu qu qu qu qu qu qu qu qu qu qu qu

The quick queen queued quietly for quoits.

Self assessment

I am confident when writing z and q:

sometimes ☐ often ☐ always ☐.

Handwriting: the letter q and the letter z don't join to the next letter. **Grammar:** prepositional phrase (for quoits); adverb (quietly). **Spelling and vocabulary**: common letter pairs; rhyme (sneeze/wheeze/freeze/breeze). **Literary elements**: alliteration.

Trace then write the anagram pairs.

horse shore

weak wake

bruise rubies

fringe finger

Watch out! Some of these letters don't join.

Write the tongue twisters.

Seth's thrifty supermarket sells thick socks.

I scream, you scream, we all scream for ice cream!

She sells sea shells by the sea shore.

The shells she sells are seashells, I'm sure.

Write a tongue twister of your own.

Handwriting: letters that don't join. **Literary elements**: anagrams; tongue twisters; alliteration.

Trace then write the anagram pairs.

garden danger   grin ring   gulp plug

night thing   jest jets   yap pay

Trace then write an anagram for each word.

flee   fringe
fits   file
fowl   softer
cafe   fare
framed   flea

Write the tongue twisters.

Granny's grey goose goes last.

A gentle judge judges justly.

Circle your five best joins on this page.

Handwriting: all joins; legibility. **Spelling and vocabulary:** soft and hard g (gentle, goose). **Literary elements**: anagrams; alliteration; tongue twisters.

Trace then write these words that are often misspelt. How fast can you write them without making any spelling mistakes and still be neat?

about almost
always answer
because before
cannot clothes
coming doctor
doesn't eighth
enough except
excited friend
guess having
heard know
laugh might
often people
quiet quite
until tonight

Don't lose those loose wheels.

Circle five words that show your writing is fluent and legible.

Handwriting: all joins; legibility. **Spelling and vocabulary**: frequently misspelt words.

Consolidation: All joins, legibility

Trace then write the compound words.

cubbyhouse steppingstone eggshell cubbyhole

piggyback grasshopper passionfruit passport

Find and write words of your own that use these double letters.

gg pp

ss bb

Trace then write.

Out of the smoggy city, across the choppy sea,

over the rugged mountains, down the slippery slope,

into the pebbly stream, through the grassy field, for

an apple.

Self assessment

My writing on this page is:

improving ☐ good ☐ fantastic ☐.

Handwriting: all joins; legibility. **Punctuation:** commas to separate phrases. **Grammar:** prepositions; prepositional phrases; adjectives; common nouns; adverb (out). **Spelling and vocabulary**: compound words (eggshell, passport).

Practise all your joins. Remember to pause if you need to and relax your hold on the pen or pencil.

Trace then write.

oe re ve we re oe re ve we oe oe re ve we re

Trace then write these adverbs.

carefully incredibly agreeably currently

entirely vertically reliably readily directly

bravely cleverly greedily prettily weekly

dreadfully drearily dreamily realistically

poetically onomatopoeically wearily wetly

Write some sentences using the adverbs above.

Handwriting: all joins; legibility. **Grammar:** adverbs ending in –ly; add –ly to change adjectives to adverbs (careful/carefully, incredible/incredibly). **Spelling and vocabulary**: change y to i to add ly (greedy/greedily); double final l before adding ly (dreadful/dreadfully).

Consolidation: All joins, legibility

Trace then write.

foe goes volcanoes tomatoes heroes

woeful whoever wrongdoer does joey

answer cobwebs welcome weary superpower

allowed sweaty tower webbed paperweight

above clever government curve forever

develop forgive invertebrate vegetable never

address admire firefighter

adventure breeze derelict

hoaxes exercise taxes

Underline any words that you could improve.

Handwriting: all joins, legibility. **Spelling and vocabulary:** compound words (firefighter, paperweight); add –es to words that end in o to make plural.

A **palindrome** is a word, phrase or sentence that reads the same forwards or backwards.

Trace then write the palindrome words.

bib dad deed
did dud eve
eye gag gig
kayak level madam
mum nan noon
peep pip pop
pup radar redder

Write the palindrome phrases and sentences. Then try writing some palindromes of your own.

race car
swap paws
snack cans
stunt nuts
Too bad I hid a boot.

Race fast, safe car.

Tick your best joins.
Put a cross next to any joins that need more practice.

Handwriting: all joins; legibility. **Grammar**: sentences. **Literary elements**: palindromes.

Trace then write each adjective. Write your own adjectives to describe how something **looks.**

grotesque multicoloured crooked sparkling dirty

Trace then write each adjective. Write your own adjectives to describe how something **sounds.**

blaring hushed squeaking raspy muffled loud

Trace then write each adjective. Write your own adjectives to describe how something **tastes.**

bitter delicious sour yummy tangy unripe

Trace then write each adjective. Write your own adjectives to describe how something **smells.**

perfumed putrid noxious musty burnt smoky

Trace then write each adjective. Write your own adjectives to describe how something **feels.**

fluffy fuzzy prickly sticky damp slippery

Handwriting: all joins; legibility. **Grammar**: adjectives. **Literary elements**: descriptions that make use of the senses.

Remember to use printing for labels.

1 Pick a genre.

scary ☐ adventure ☐ historical ☐

mystery ☐ fantasy ☐ funny ☐

2 Draw a map of a possible setting for a story in your chosen genre.

3 Add labels. Include labels to describe what you might see, hear, smell, feel and taste if you were standing in this setting.

Self assessment

My printing on this page is:

improving ☐ good ☐ fantastic ☐.

Handwriting: printing to label maps and diagrams. **Literary elements**: genre; setting; descriptions.

Writing that all has the same slope looks neater and is easier to read.

An **anagram** is a word or phrase made by changing the order of the letters in another word or phrase.

Trace then write the anagrams.

astronomers = no more stars

the eyes = they see

mummy = my mum

the countryside = no city dust here

conversation = voices rant on

twelve plus one = eleven plus two

vacation time = I am not active

My writing slopes in the same direction:

sometimes ☐ often ☐ always ☐.

Handwriting: all joins; consistent slope; legibility. **Grammar**: phrases. **Literary elements**: anagrams.

Trace then write.

said
he
she
they
his
her
their
your
can
could
will
from
where
when
which
who
what

These words are from a list of 100 most used words that make up about half of all reading and writing.

You'll need to write these words often. Practise writing them as quickly as you can while still being neat.

Self assessment

On each line:
Draw a star above the word you wrote the fastest.
Tick the word you wrote the neatest.

Handwriting: speed and fluency; legibility. **Spelling and vocabulary**: common words.

Consolidation: All joins

Trace then write the different ways to say 'said'.

announced argued asked babbled

barked bawled bellowed bleated

blurted called chattered cheered

croaked drawled growled grumbled

hissed muttered piped quavered

ranted roared shouted sighed

snapped sobbed stammered whimpered

There's nothing wrong with using the word said.

BUT I LIKE TO YELL!

And I like to whisper.

Write your own words to use instead of 'said'.

Handwriting: all joins. **Grammar**: saying verbs. **Spelling and vocabulary**: synonyms. **Literary elements**: words for 'said'.

Remember to sit comfortably.

Interjections are words that show emotion or feelings. They can stand alone.

Trace then write the interjections for each emotion. Write one in each speech bubble in the picture.

angry: grrr agh humph

happy: bravo eureka yippee

sad: aw alas drat

worried: uh oh oops oh no

questioning: hey eh huh

scared: eek ahhhh yikes

relieved: phew golly whoa

Trace then write a sentence to follow each interjection.

Eek!

Yippee!

Handwriting: all joins. **Grammar**: interjections.

Consolidation: All joins

Trace the nouns for items in the kitchen. Then, for each letter of the alphabet, write your own noun for something in your home.

almonds bok choy curry dumplings

a b c d

eggflip forks garbage herbs

e f g h

ice juice knives lemons

i j k l

mushrooms nuts oranges plates

m n o p

quinces radishes sausages tangerines

q r s t

utensils vegetables watermelon

u v w

toxic mould yoghurt zucchinis

x y z

Choose four kitchen items. Write them here with an adjective for each one, for example, 'sour lemons'.

Circle five words that show your writing is fluent and legible.

Handwriting: all joins. **Grammar:** nouns; adjectives. **Spelling and vocabulary**: different types of plurals –es (radishes), –s (lemons); no change from singular to plural (bok choy, garbage, ice, yoghurt, mould).

Remember to keep your letter shape, size, slope, and spacing consistent.

Trace then write the thinking verbs.

hope hoped wished wondered believed knew

Trace then write.

Thomas sat in the doctor's waiting room, trying not to panic about his arm. It wasn't looking good. A red stain was seeping through the bandage. Oops, thought Thomas. I think I used too much jam.

Cross out the words that don't apply.
I need to work on my letter shapes, slope, spacing, size.

Handwriting: all joins. **Grammar**: thinking verbs (thought, think); apostrophe for possession (doctor's); proper noun (Thomas); prepositional phrases (in the doctor's waiting room). **Spelling and vocabulary**: apostrophe for contraction (wasn't); homophone (too/to/two). **Literary elements:** third person narrative; point of view; quote from *Doubting Thomas* by Morris Gleitzman (2006).

Trace then write.

sch scr spl spr shr sph squ str thr

sch school scr scream spl splat

spr sprint shr shriek sph sphere

squ square str straight thr through

Find and write a word of your own for each letter cluster.

sch scr spl

spr shr sph

squ str thr

Trace then write.

Characters in scary movies

shriek and scream.

Put a cross next to any joins that you could improve.

Handwriting: all joins. **Grammar:** saying verbs (shriek, scream). **Spelling and vocabulary**: three letter consonant blends 'spl', 'spr'.

Trace then write.

au aw or ai ay ea ee ei er oa au aw

ow eu ew ey ie oi oo ou ow oy ow eu

au automatic aw awful or short sport fort

ai straight ay day slay ea meat cheat bleat

ee cheek ei eight er germ oa boat oath

ow power shower eu eureka ew drew slew

ey prey grey ie pie die oi toil boil avoid

oo scoot ou shout oy boy

Write words that rhyme.

port	pleat	flew
stay	tower	spoil
lie	peek	float

Handwriting: all joins. **Spelling and vocabulary:** digraphs for vowel sounds 'au', 'ai', 'oi', 'ea', 'ee', 'oa', 'ei', 'ie', 'eu', 'ou', 'oo', 'aw', 'or', 'er', 'ew', 'ow', 'ey', 'ay', 'oy'.

Consolidation: All joins

Trace then write.

first second third fourth fifth sixth

seventh eighth ninth tenth hundredth

tle castle rustle dge dodge ght night flight

nk stink tion nation motion lk stalk talk

Write words of your own which use the letter patterns.

tle	dge	ght
nk	tion	lk

Choose a homophone from the box for each word below.

whale would know eight flower through hair
creak steel boy choose fur stalk piece sale

peace	steal	no
ate	wood	hare
wail	flour	creek
threw	buoy	chews
fir	stork	sail

Handwriting: all joins. **Spelling and vocabulary**: homophones; letter patterns –tle, –dge, –ght, –nk, –tion, –lk.

Trace. Then choose a prefix from the box to make an antonym.

un im ir il dis

___known	___possible	___tidy
___practical	___natural	___obedient
___intentional	___stable	___like
___qualify	___believable	___agree
___approve	___able	___regular
___rational	___mature	___obey

Trace. Then add a suffix from the box to each word.
Some words might be able to use more than one suffix.

ful less able

hope	care	paper
help	effort	waste
wish	thought	dread
approach	fear	answer
spot	mind	count
fix	kiss	taste

Trace. Then write these words with silent letters.

thumb	scene	gnaw
knock	autumn	whistle
guitar	guess	wrestle

Handwriting: all joins. **Spelling and vocabulary**: antonyms; negative prefixes un–, im–, ir–, il–, dis–; suffixes –ful, –less, –able; silent letters (thumb, scene, gnaw, knock, autumn, whistle, guitar, guess, wrestle).

A **pangram** is a sentence that uses every letter of the alphabet. You can use letters more than once.

Trace then write these pangrams.

The wolf just kept dozing very quietly in a crumpled box.

The mad taxi driver wove quickly past the frisky zebra crossing the road.

A big killer ox squashed the very cute jumping frogs as they did a waltz.

Write a pangram of your own.

Cross out the words that don't apply.
I need to work on my letter shapes, slope, spacing, size.

Handwriting: all joins. **Literary elements:** pangrams.

Trace then write these sentences about classic stories.

Make sure your writing arm and hand can move freely. Keep your pencil or pen hold relaxed and flexible.

The children entered Narnia

through a wardrobe in the spare room.

En-garde

A cyclone whirled Dorothy

and Toto to the Land of Oz.

Gulliver was washed ashore in Lilliput.

Peter Pan and Tinkerbell flew to Neverland.

Alice fell into a rabbit-hole and

discovered Wonderland.

Write a sentence of your own that tells how a story character entered a fantasy world.

Handwriting: all joins. **Grammar:** proper nouns (Narnia, Dorothy, Toto, Land of Oz, Gulliver, Lilliput, Peter Pan, Tinkerbell, Neverland, Alice, Wonderland); prepositional phrases (through a wardrobe, in the spare room); verbs (whirled, was washed). **Literary elements**: fantasy genre, characters and settings; entering fantasy worlds; references to *The Lion, the Witch and the Wardrobe* by C S Lewis (1950), *The Wonderful Wizard of Oz* by L Frank Baum (1900), *Gulliver's Travels* by Jonathan Swift (1726), *Peter Pan* by JM Barrie (1911), *Alice's Adventures in Wonderland* by Lewis Carroll (1865). (Note, these books have all been made into films.)

Consolidation: All joins

Trace then write the similes.

as scarce as hen's teeth

as bold as brass

as clear as mud

as nutty as a fruit cake

You have no teeth!

Trace then write the lines from a playscript.

Scene: Shaggy man and Button-bright face the Scoodlers.

Shaggy man: What do you want?

Scoodlers (yelling, pointing): You!

Shaggy man: What do you want us for?

Scoodlers (shouting): Soup!

Button-bright (crying): Don't want to be soup.

Handwriting: all joins. **Grammar:** questions; exclamation; statement; proper nouns (Shaggy man, Scoodlers, Button-bright). **Punctuation:** colons; brackets; exclamation marks; question marks. **Literary elements**: similes; tongue-in-cheek humour; irony; colloquialism; stage directions; characters; playscript adapted from Chapter 9, 'Facing the Scoodlers', from *The Road to Oz* by L Frank Baum (1909).

Some words used in English come from First Nations languages.

Trace then write these words for plants and animals.

kangaroo bogong wallaroo wallaby dingo

galah currawong bunyip boobook bilby

pademelon quokka quoll waratah wombat

yabby kookaburra

wobbegong numbat

brolga taipan

budgerigar myall mallee

mulga potoroo witchetty koala drongo quandong

barramundi coolabah kurrajong gang-gang

Handwriting: all joins. **Spelling and vocabulary**: etymology; words in English from First Nations languages.

Write the quote.

In the High and Far-Off Times the Elephant, O Best Beloved, had no trunk. He had only a blackish, bulgy nose, as big as a boot, that he could wriggle about from side to side; but he couldn't pick up things with it.

Rate your writing out of 10:

fluency ____ speed ____ legibility ____.

Handwriting: fluency; speed and legibility. **Grammar**: adjectives (blackish, bulgy); noun group (a blackish, bulgy nose). **Literary elements**: quote from 'The Elephant's Child' from *Just So Stories* by Rudyard Kipling (1902); simile (as big as a boot).

Write. Focus on shape, slope and size.

There was a man in our town,

And he was wondrous wise;

He jumped into a bramble bush,

And scratched out both his eyes;

And when he saw his eyes were out,

With all his might and main

He jumped into another bush,

And scratched them in again.

Draw a star next to the line that shows your best writing. (Think about shape, slope and letter sizes.)

Handwriting: letter shape; slope; size. **Literary elements**: Mother Goose rhyme; idiom 'might and main' meaning 'with all his strength or power' – relevant to time when Mother Goose stories were first published (1695).

There's a very funny insect
that you do not often spy,
And it isn't quite a spider
and it isn't quite a fly;
It is something like a beetle,
and a little like a bee,
But nothing like a woolly grub
that climbs upon a tree.
Its name is quite a hard one,
but you'll learn it soon, I hope.
So try: Tri- Tri-anti-wonti
Triantiwontigongolope.

The Triantiwontigongolope

Write the poem. Draw a triantiwontigongolope in the box above.

Handwriting: all joins. **Literary elements**: made-up words; poetry; quote from 'The Triantiwontigongolope', from *A Book for Kids* by CJ Dennis (1921).

Some place names in Australia come from Australian First Nations languages.

Print the labels on the map.

1 Mundaring
2 Karratha
3 Pilbara
4 Jabiru
5 Kalgoorlie
6 Coolgardie
7 Yulara
8 Nhulunbuy
9 Aurukun
10 Tanunda
11 Cocklebiddy
12 Biloela
13 Noosa
14 Maroochydore
15 Currumbin
16 Arakoon
17 Wilcannia
18 Dubbo
19 Uralla
20 Turramurra
21 Parramatta
22 Ballarat
23 Thirroul
24 Geelong
25 Wonthaggi
26 Canberra

Research place names in Tasmania that come from First Nations languages. Write one on the line. Use an arrow to point to its location on the map.

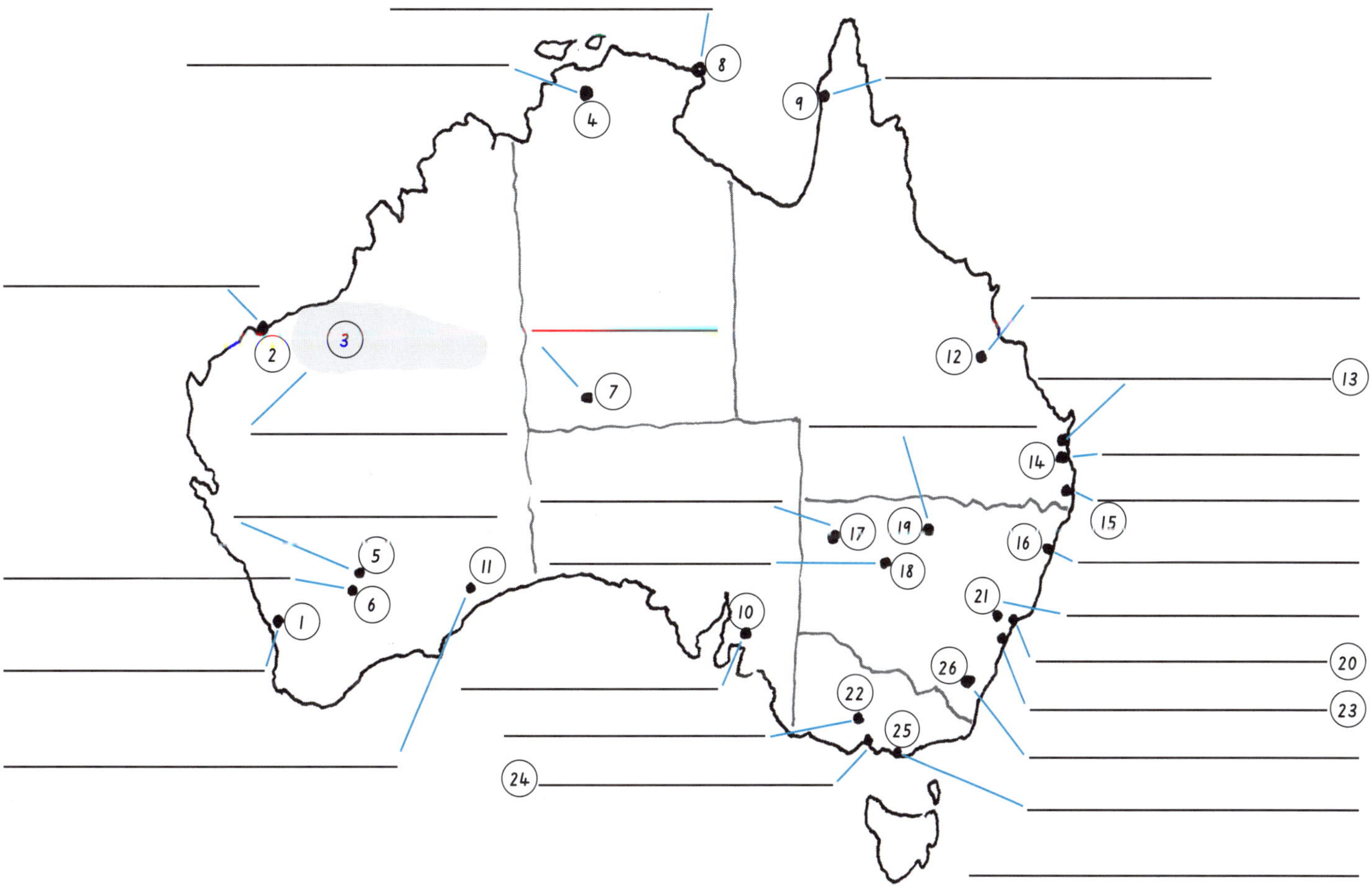

Handwriting: using printing to label maps and diagrams. **Spelling and vocabulary**: etymology; Australian First Nations languages.

Complete the crime scene report to investigate what happened to Humpty Dumpty. Did Humpty fall or was it foul play?

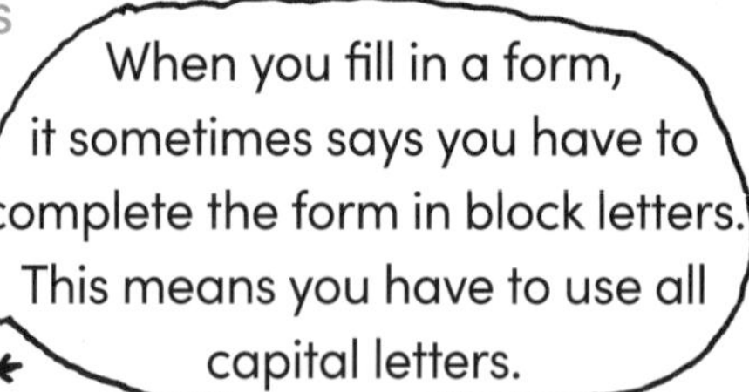

CRIME SCENE REPORT TO BE COMPLETED IN BLOCK LETTERS	
TYPE OF CRIME	
WHERE CRIME TOOK PLACE	
TIME CRIME TOOK PLACE	
VICTIM DETAILS	
DESCRIPTION OF CRIME SCENE	
EVIDENCE COLLECTED	
WITNESS NAME	
WITNESS STATEMENT	

Handwriting: upper-case (capital) letters. **Literary elements**: common expression (foul play).

Here are some new lines to try.

Remember to keep your letters a consistent size and in correct proportion.

Trace then write the sentences. Finish each sentence with a character name from the box.

Rapunzel	Goldilocks	The Wolf	Jack	Baby Bear

"Oh! Someone ate my porridge," cried

"I'll blow your house down," shouted

"Oops! I broke the chair," said

"I'll hang down my hair," said

"Yikes! The Giant is coming!" yelled

Write a sentence of your own for each character in the box.

Cinderella	The Little Mermaid	
Red Riding Hood	Grandma	Aladdin

Handwriting: introducing 8mm blue-lined paper; maintaining letter size and proportion without guidelines. **Grammar:** interjections; exclamations; dialogue; saying verbs (cried, shouted, yelled, said); proper nouns (Goldilocks, Cinderella, Aladdin). **Punctuation:** quotation marks; exclamation marks. **Literary elements**: fairy tales; story characters.

Trace then write. Finish the speech bubbles.

The solemn gnome hurt his thumb whilst making

fudge on Wednesday. He had to guard the dessert from

the naughty knight at the castle, so he climbed a cliff

and hid it under some thistles. He ate the fudge after

an hour, leaving no crumbs.

Handwriting: 8mm lines; maintaining letter size and proportion without guidelines. **Spelling and vocabulary:** words with silent letters (solemn, gnome, thumb, Wednesday, guard, naughty, knight, castle, climbed, thistles, hour, crumbs); fudge uses dge to make a j sound; desert/dessert often confused. **Literary elements**: fantasy characters (gnome, knight, dragon).

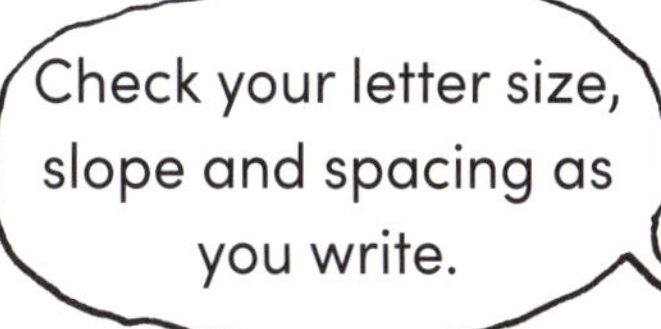

Trace then write.

The accused biter hopped into a tiny tinny. He took his rabbit and his kitten, too. All of a sudden his rudder shuddered having jammed into an alligator. It was difficult to steer and he slammed into some jagged rocks. His canny granny pulled his boat to shore. He commented, later, that he'd seen the error of his ways.

Self assessment

Rate your writing out of 10:

fluency ____ speed ____ legibility ____.

Handwriting: 8mm lines; maintaining letter size and proportion without guidelines. **Spelling and vocabulary:** common mistakes (tiny/tinny, hopped/hoped); rhyme (rudder/shudder, slammed/jammed).

Check your letter size, slope and spacing as you write. Try to write as quickly as you can but make sure your writing is still legible.

Trace then write this stanza from a Henry Lawson poem.

It leapt across the flaming streams
And raced the pastures through;
It climbed the trees, and lit the boughs,
And fierce and fiercer grew.
The bees fell stifled in the smoke
Or perished in their hives,
And with the stock the kangaroos
Went flying for their lives.

My letter size is consistent:

sometimes ☐ often ☐ always ☐.

Handwriting: 8mm lines; maintaining letter size and proportion without guidelines. **Spelling and vocabulary:** 'ough' (through, bough). **Literary elements:** poetry; quote from 'The Fire at Ross's Farm', published in *The Days When The World Was Wide* by Henry Lawson (1900).

Write the limericks in your best joined writing. Draw an illustration for each limerick.

There was an old man in a barge,
Whose nose was exceedingly large;
But in fishing by night, it supported a light,
Which helped that old man in a barge.

There was a young lady of Greenwich,
Whose garments were border'd with Spinach;
But a large spotty Calf bit her shawl quite in half,
Which alarmed that young lady of Greenwich.

Handwriting: 8mm lines; maintaining letter size and proportion without guidelines. **Grammar:** possessive pronoun (whose). **Punctuation:** upper-case (capital) letter to start each line of a poem; semicolons. **Literary elements:** limericks; 'There Was an Old Man in a Barge', 'There was a Young Lady of Greenwich', from *More Nonsense, Pictures, Rhymes, Botany &c* by Edward Lear (1872).

A signature needs to be the same each time you write it. It needs to be quick and easy to write.

Experiment with different ways to sign your name.

Choose your favourite signature. Practise writing it on the lines.
Try to write each signature exactly the same.

Circle your favourite signature.

Handwriting: developing your own personal style.

Collect autographs from your classmates and teachers.

An **autograph** is someone's signature.

You can stamp and rage,
I'm still first in this page.

You'd better write fast,
or you'll be the last!

Assessment: Progressive speed and fluency trials

Have a classmate time you as you rewrite the sentence from the box. Use all the joins you have learned. Make sure you write as fluently and legibly as you can.

> Grumpy dancers caught a quick taxi to Wonthaggi to juggle volleyballs for the crazy human circus.

Assessment 1

Date ____________________ Time ________ minutes ________ seconds

Assessment 2

Date ____________________ Time ________ minutes ________ seconds

Assessment 3

Date ____________________ Time ________ minutes ________ seconds

Assessment 4

Date ____________________ Time ________ minutes ________ seconds

Assessment 5

Date ____________________ Time ________ minutes ________ seconds

Handwriting: writing at speed but with fluency and legibility. **Grammar:** adjectives (grumpy, quick); classifying adjective (human); common nouns (dancers, volleyballs, taxi, circus); proper noun (Wonthaggi); doing verbs (caught, juggle). **Spelling and vocabulary:** The word Wonthaggi means home and is from the Boon Wurrung language. **Literary elements:** pangram.

Assessment: Progressive self-assessment

Read each of the criteria listed below. When you think you have achieved each one, write the date and sign off.

- My letters are consistently the right shape and an even size. ☐ ____________________
- My letters are a consistent height. ☐ ____________________
- My letters sit on the line correctly. ☐ ____________________
- My descenders are a consistent length. ☐ ____________________
- My letters have the same slope. ☐ ____________________
- The space between my letters is regular. ☐ ____________________
- The space between my words is regular. ☐ ____________________
- My joins are fluent. ☐ ____________________
- Others can easily read my handwriting. ☐ ____________________
- My writing is automatic. (I don't have to think too hard about how to join the letters fluently.) ☐ ____________________
- I can write quickly when I need to and my fast writing is legible to others. ☐ ____________________
- I have developed confidence and pride in my handwriting style. ☐ ____________________

Have you signed off on each of the criteria?

You've successfully completed your journey to the worlds of FLUENCY and LEGIBILITY.